ONE POTATO

Songs For Early Learners

From the Big Banana Company

Songs by Rebecca Front
and Hugh Kermode
With puzzles by Catherine Addis

Illustrated by Fred Apps

Recorded in BBC Studios, Bush House
Studio Manager: Simon Morecroft

This book belongs to:

____

Where's the banana?
There's a banana on each song page
- can you find it?

One Potato from the Big Banana Company is a co-production between BBC English Radio and SIRS Editions-Disques BBC (France).

ISBN: 1-85497-275-8

Published by: BBC English, PO Box 76, Bush House, London WC2B 4PH/SIRS Editions-Disques BBC (France), 8 Rue de Berri, 75008 Paris.

With thanks to Miti Adhikari, Andrew Ross Aird, Carrie Dunton, Henri Fulton, Jon Magnusson and Andrew Phillips. Special thanks to Mike Engels and Simon Morecroft.

ONE POTATO
Songs And Games
THE BIG BANANA CO
BBC ENGLISH

ONE BANANA

One banana, two bananas,
three bananas, four;
Five bananas, six bananas,
seven bananas, more!
Eight bananas, nine bananas,
ten bananas again.

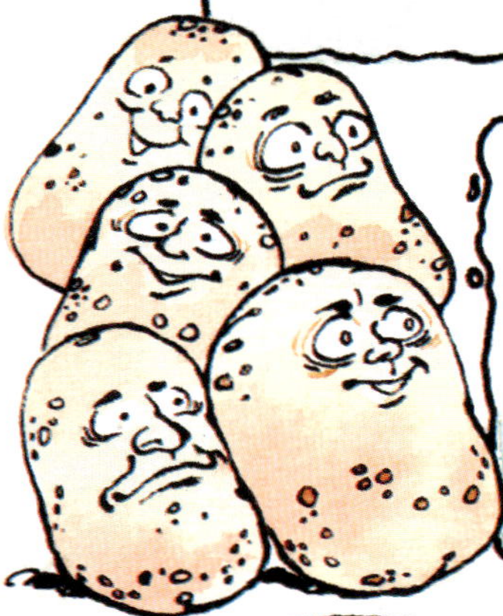

One potato, two potatoes,
three potatoes, four;
Five potatoes, six potatoes,
seven potatoes, more!
Eight potatoes, nine potatoes,
ten potatoes again.

One tomato, two tomatoes,
three tomatoes, four;
Five tomatoes, six tomatoes,
seven tomatoes, more!
Eight tomatoes, nine tomatoes,
ten tomatoes again.

One banana, two bananas,
three bananas, four;
Five bananas, six bananas,
seven bananas, more!
Eight bananas, nine bananas,
ten bananas again.

How many?

1  one potato

2  two bananas

3  ______________

4  ______________

5  ______________

6  ______________

7  ______________

8  ______________

9  ______________

10  ______________

ROUND THE MULBERRY BUSH

Here we go round the
mulberry bush,
The mulberry bush? The
mulberry bush.
Here we go round the
mulberry bush,
On a cold and frosty
morning.

This is the way we brush
our teeth,
Brush our teeth? Brush
our teeth.
This is the way we brush
our teeth,
On a cold and frosty
morning.

This is the way we wash
our hair.
Wash our hair? Wash
our hair.
This is the way we wash
our hair,
On a cold and frosty
morning.

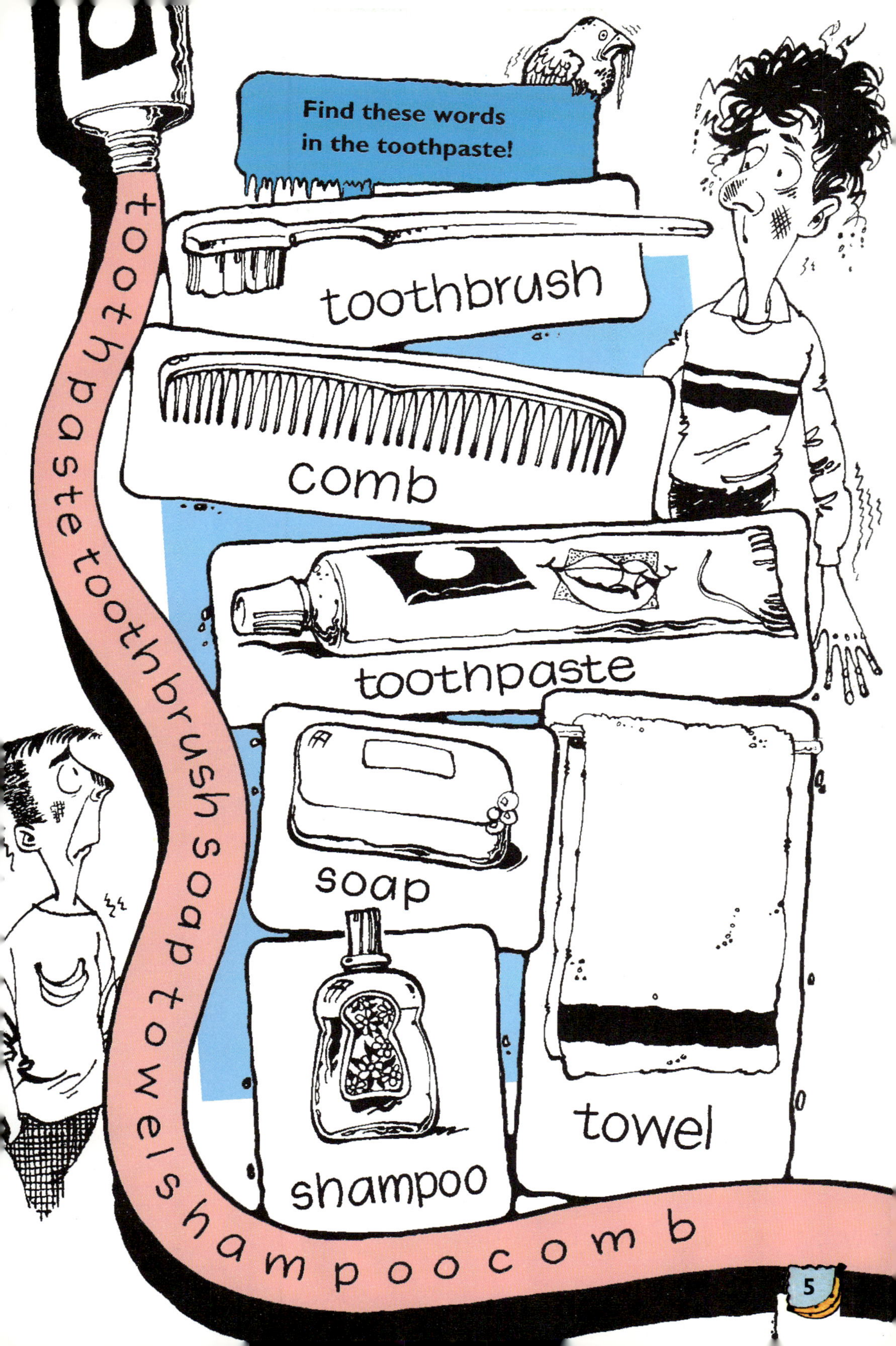
Find these words
in the toothpaste!
toothbrush
comb
toothpaste
soap
shampoo
towel
toothpastetoothbrushsoaptowelshampoocomb

TEN GREEN BOTTLES

Ten green bottles, standing on the wall.
Ten green bottles, standing on the wall.
And if one green bottle should accidentally fall,
There'd be nine bottles, standing on the wall.

Write the first letters of these words on the wall.
What do you see?

Lavender's Blue

What colour are the flowers?

Colour them in.

Join the dots to find something a King or Queen wears.

CROWN

ONE TWO BUCKLE MY SHOE
ONE TWO
buckle my shoe,
THREE FOUR
knock at the door,
FIVE SIX
pick up sticks,
SEVEN EIGHT
open the gate,
NINE TEN
do it again.

Add up these sums. Write the answer in numbers and words.

January February March April May June July August September October November December

How many months are there in a year? ______________________

How many brothers and sisters have you got? ______________________

Monday Tuesday Wednesday Thursday Friday Saturday Sunday

How many days are there in a week? ______________________

What is the number of your house? ______________________

____

I'M A LITTLE TEAPOT

I'm a little teapot short and stout,
Here's my handle, here's my spout.
When the water's boiling, hear me shout,
Tip me up and pour me out!

Put the words into the chart. Something you drink will appear!

Put these pictures in the right order and make a cup of tea.

HICKORY DICKORY DOCK

Hickory, dickory, dock,
The mouse ran up the clock.
The clock struck one,
The mouse ran down,
Hickory, dickory, dock.

Hickory, dickory, dock,
The mouse ran up the clock.
The clock struck one,
The mouse ran down,
Hickory, dickory, dock.

Hickory, dickory, dock,
The mouse ran up the clock.
The clock struck one,
The mouse ran down,
Hickory, dickory, dock.

VERA'S DAY

7.15
What time does Vera get up?
What time does she get home?
11.30
What time does she go to bed?
What time does she go to work?
What time does she have lunch?
Write these times onto the digital watch.
Ten past one
1.10
Five past nine
Quarter to three
Ten past midday

OLD MACDONALD

Old MacDonald had a farm,
E I E I O.
And on that farm he had a cow,
E I E I O.
With a **moo moo** here,
And a **moo moo** there,
Here a **moo,** there a **moo,**
Everywhere a **moo moo**.
Old MacDonald had a farm,
E I E I O.

Old MacDonald had a farm,
E I E I O.
And on that farm he had a pig,
E I E I O.
With a **oink oink** here,
And a **oink oink** there,
Here a **oink,** there a **oink,**
Everywhere a **oink oink**.
Old MacDonald had a farm,
E I E I O.

Old MacDonald had a farm,
E I E I O.
And on that farm he had a duck,
E I E I O.
With a **quack quack** here,
And a **quack quack** there,
Here a **quack,** there a **quack,**
Everywhere a **quack quack**.
Old MacDonald had a farm,
E I E I O.

Old MacDonald had a farm,
E I E I O.
And on that farm he had a dog,
E I E I O.
With a **woof woof** here,
And a **woof woof** there,
Here a **woof,** there a **woof,**
Everywhere a **woof woof**.
Old MacDonald had a farm,
E I E I O.

Old MacDonald had a farm,
E I E I O.
And on that farm he had some animals,
E I E I O.
With a ..here, and a ..there, here a ..,
there a .., everywhere a ...
Old MacDonald had a farm,
E I E I O.

Some things are missing from this farmyard scene! Draw them in.

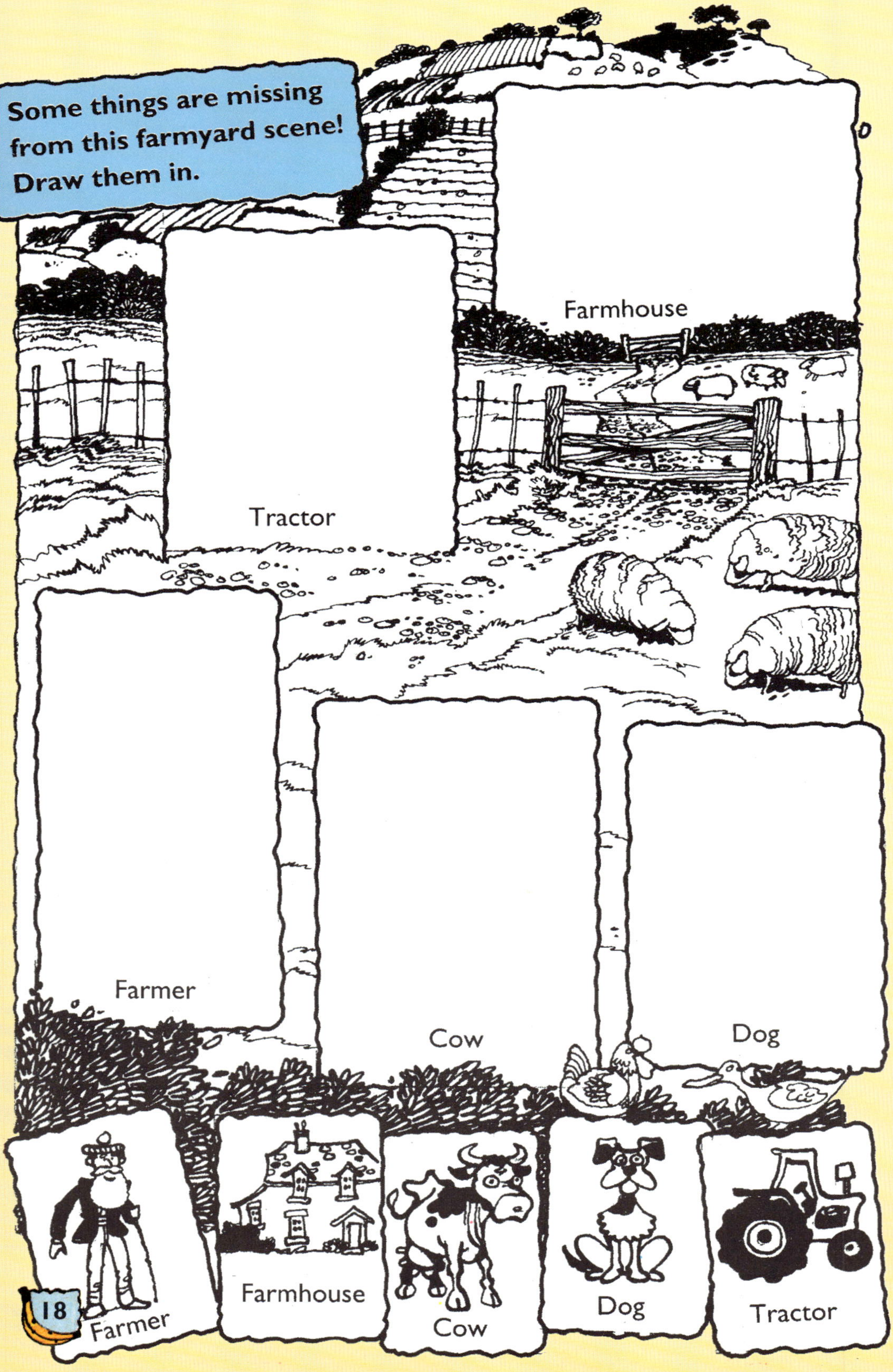

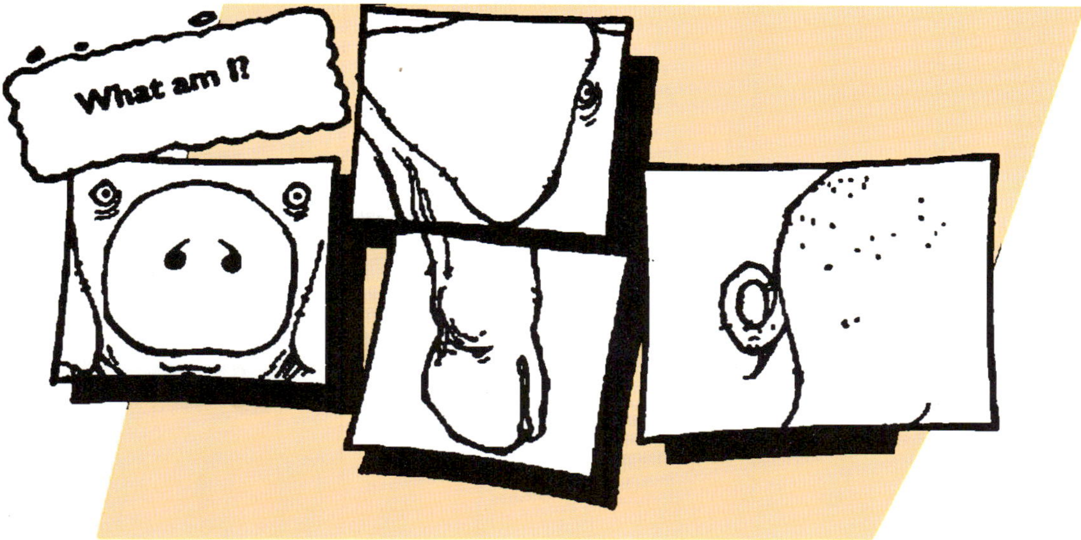
What am I?

Twinkle Twinkle Little Star

Twinkle, twinkle, little star,
How I wonder what you are.
Up above the world so high,
Like a diamond in the sky.
Twinkle, twinkle, little star,
How I wonder what you are.

Imagine you are looking down at these objects from the sky.

What are they?

Write the names here:

Match up these stars to find some things in the sky.

I found these words:

____

____

____

____

____

THE LITTLE TURTLE

There was a little turtle,
He lived in a box,
He swam in a puddle,
He climbed on the rocks.

He snapped at a mosquito,
He snapped at a flea,
He snapped at a minnow,
And he snapped at me!

He caught the mosquito,
He caught the flea,
He caught the minnow,
But he didn't catch me!

There was a little turtle,
He lived in a box,
He swam in a puddle,
He climbed on the rocks.

Can you find five words from the song on the turtle? The words can go →↘↓

I found these words:

Rocks

______

______

______

______

What is the turtle doing?

a.

He's Swimming

e.

He's ______

b.

He's ______

c.

He's ______

d

He's ______

Join the dots to find two more insects the turtle likes.

SPIDER

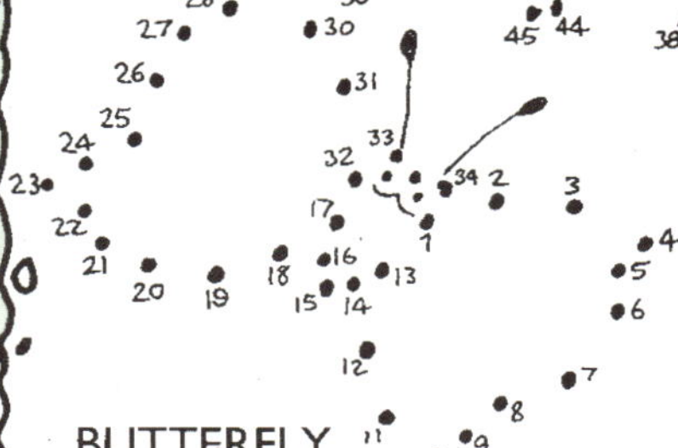

BUTTERFLY

LONDON'S BURNING
London's burning,
London's burning,
Fetch the engines,
Fetch the engines.
Fire, Fire!
Fire, Fire!
Pour on water!
Pour on water!

Look at the picture. Can you find these things that begin with **F**?

fire
fireman
fire engine
five o'clock
fly
flag
fruit shop
fish
flowers

ROW YOUR BOAT
Row, row,
Row your
boat,
Gently down the stream.
Merrily, merrily,
Merrily, merrily,
Life is
but a dream.

What can you see? Name it.

H _ _ S _

BI _ _ C _ _

_ OW

FL _ _ ERS

CAS _ _ _ _

T _ EES

T _ _ _ _

Match the word with the picture.

lake

sea

pond

puddle

HEAD, SHOULDERS, KNEES AND TOES

Get your hands ready and stand in line,
Get your hands ready, if you've got the time.
We're going to do this dance everyone,
So get ready to do it with MC Pendulum!
Hello everybody, h-h-hello everybody!
Hello everybody, h-h-hello everybody!

Touch your head,
your shoulders, knees and toes
(knees and toes).
Come on head,
shoulders, knees and toes
(knees and toes).
And your eyes,
your ears, your mouth
and your nose.
Touch your head,
your shoulders, knees and toes
(knees and toes).

Head, shoulders, knees and toes,
Head, shoulders, knees and toes,
Eyes and ears and mouth and nose,
Head, shoulders, knees and toes.

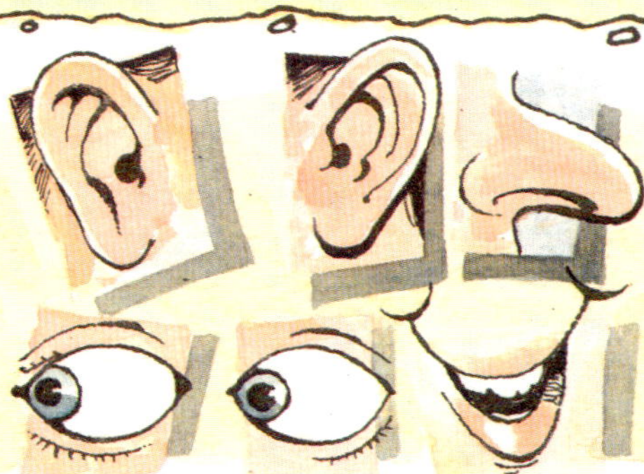

Put the right number next to the word.

hand ...
eyes ...
elbow ...
finger ...
nose ...
leg ...
stomach ...
hair ...
neck ...
foot ...

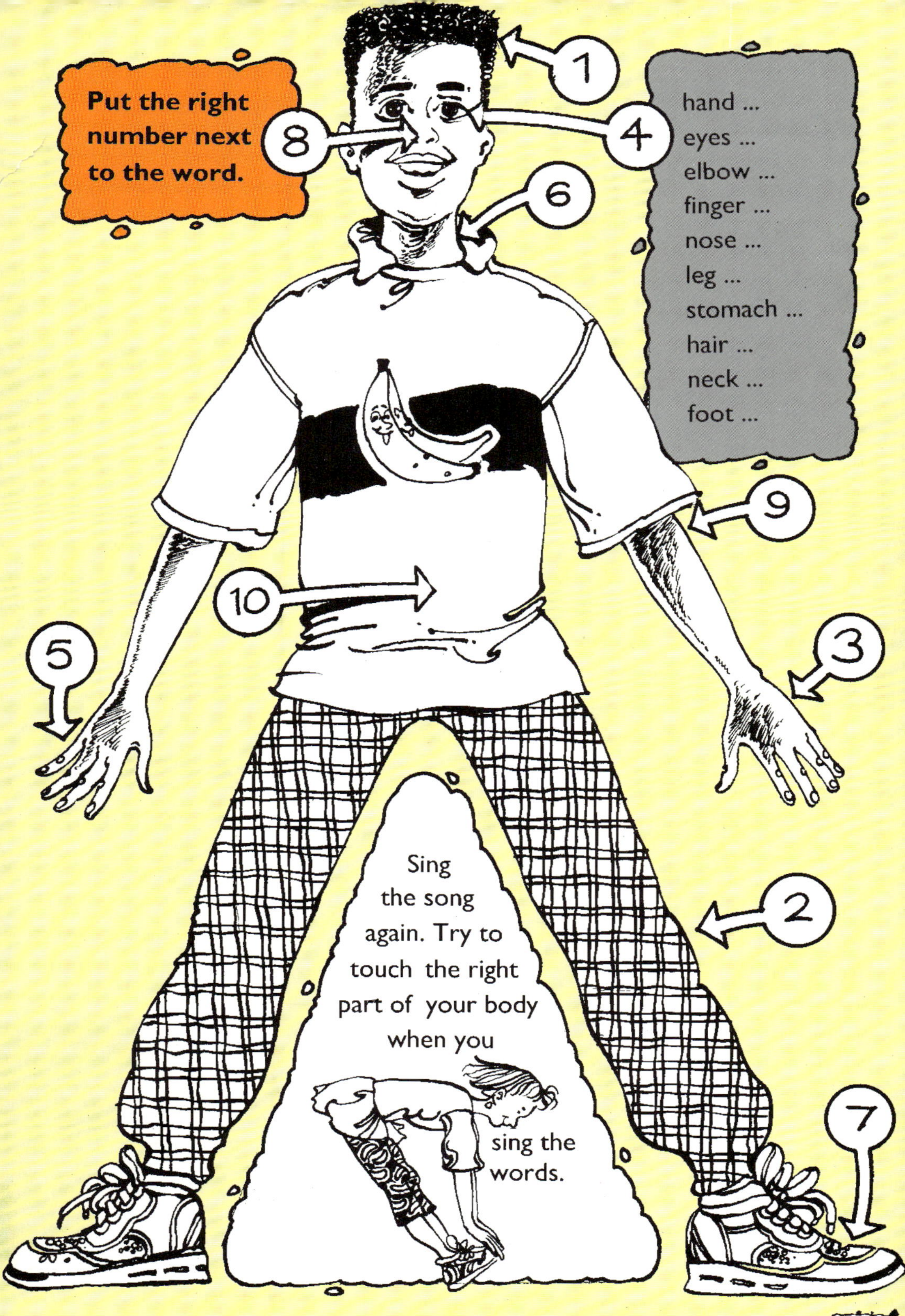

Sing the song again. Try to touch the right part of your body when you sing the words.

BOBBY SHAFTOE

Bobby Shaftoe's gone to sea,
Silver buckles at his knee.

Bobby Shaftoe's bright and fair,
Combing down his yellow hair,

He'll come back and marry me,
Bonny Bobby Shaftoe.

I'll go with him everywhere,
Bonny Bobby Shaftoe.

Here's Bobby Shaftoe. Use your favourite colours to colour him in.
What colours did you choose?
His trousers are
His hat is
His shirt is
His shoes are
His socks are
His scarf is
His belt is

INCY WINCY SPIDER

I want to tell you all about Incy,
'Cos Incy is a friend of mine.
Incy Wincy, Incy Wincy spider,
The hero of a nursery rhyme.

Incy lived a boring life,
In the bottom of a watering can.
He wanted some adventure,
And this, this is how he began.

Incy Wincy spider climbed the
water spout,
Then along came the rain and
washed poor Incy out.
Then along came the sun and
dried up all the rain,
And Incy Wincy spider,
He climbed the spout, he
climbed the spout,
He climbed the spout again.

What's the weather like?

It's ___Sunny___

It's ___wet___

It's ___windy___

It's ___cold___

Put the right number on the picture.

1. umbrella
2. sunglasses
3. scart
4. shoes
5. sweater
6. swimming costume

What's the weather like where you live?

In May it's ______________

In December it's ______________

In September it's ______________

In July it's ______________

BYE BYE!

We hope you enjoyed these songs
from the Big Banana Company.
Did you find all the bananas?

See you soon!